Hidden Critters

Can You Find Them All?

Stan Tekiela

Adventure Publications
Cambridge, Minnesota

DEDICATION

To all of the amazing wildlife in the world. You continue to amaze and delight me.

Photos by Stan Tekiela

Edited by Sandy Livoti

Cover and book design by Jonathan Norberg

10 9 8 7 6 5 4

Hidden Critters: Can You Find Them All?

Published by Adventure Publications
An imprint of AdventureKEEN
310 Garfield Street South
Cambridge, Minnesota 55008
(800) 678-7006
www.adventurepublications.net

Printed in China
ISBN 978-1-59193-812-5 (pbk.)

Hidden Critters

I am well hidden in green fields,
even though I'm brown.

I live underground in prairies,
and I'm said to be wise.

My big yellow eyes help me see
when I fly at night.

Do you see
me hidden?
Who am I?

I'M AN OWL!

The **burrowing owl** is tiny with long bare legs and strong feet. It digs out a burrow in the dirt, using its legs and feet like a pair of shovels. The underground home is a safe place for this critter to hide. Outside, it decorates the entrance with animal poop. **YUCK!** This draws in bugs to eat.

I'm plain and mostly gray,
but I'm hidden in this
colorful tundra.

My family and I live in forests,
mountains and other wild places.

I look like a large, furry dog,
and I'm famous for my howling.

Do you see
me hidden?
Who am I?

I'M A WOLF!

The gray wolf can be gray, black or even white. No matter the color, it's a great hunter and doesn't try to hide. Families are important to wolves, just like for you and me. Mom and Dad are the leaders of their group, called a pack. When they bring food home to their den, the hungry pups get to eat first. **YUMMY!**

I'm seen a lot in trees, but I'm not a bird.

I have a flat, furry tail, and I feed on acorns.

People think I fly, but I only glide from tree to tree.

Do you see me hidden? Who am I?

I'M A
FLYING SQUIRREL!

Almost everyone has seen squirrels, but it's much harder to spot a **southern flying squirrel**. That's because they come out at night, when we're sleeping! Flying squirrels don't actually fly, but they're experts at gliding. They scamper to a treetop, launch into the air and glide to another tree. **WHEE!**

I am long and leathery, and I have a big mouth. But I'm hard to see in water.

I hunt with just my eyes and nose above the surface.

I like it hot! Sometimes I rest on land and warm up in the sun.

Do you see me hidden? Who am I?

I'M AN ALLIGATOR!

The **American alligator** can grow up to 15 feet long and weigh over 500 pounds. It's a strong and clever hunter. To hide, it floats and stays very still in the water. When something to eat wanders nearby, **CHOMP!** With lightning speed and powerful jaws, it snaps up dinner.

I am tiny and brown, so I can hide without trying.

I live in forests, where I creep up big trees.

I find bugs to eat with my beak, and I fly with my wings.

Do you see me hidden? Who am I?

I'M A BIRD!

The brown creeper is a forest bird. It blends in on tree bark, where it hunts for food. It has a long tail with tiny spines underneath. The spines help it cling to trees. The brown creeper flies to the bottom of a tree and creeps its way up the trunk. **COOL!** This is how it searches for spider eggs, caterpillars and other treasures to eat.

My fur is snowy white in winter and brown in summer.

I have very short legs, but I'm super fast when I run!

I am skinny, and I wiggle into small places to hunt.

Do you see me hidden? Who am I?

I'M A WEASEL!

The **short-tailed weasel** is one of the few animals that change color. It is brown all summer. In winter, it becomes mostly white. So it's hard to see on snowy ground. This small critter hunts for other animals. It squeezes into tight places under shrubs and darts into underground burrows. It may be little, but it sure is fast. **ZING!**

I am green and slippery, with strong hind legs.

I catch bugs to eat with my long tongue.

When I call out from my pond, I'm loud and croaky.

Do you see me hidden? Who am I?

I'M A FROG!

The American bullfrog is one of the largest frogs you'll ever see. It croaks out a loud "rum, rum, rum!" Lots of critters like to eat bullfrogs. So it sits very still near green plants in the pond. This makes it hard to notice. At night it becomes active and hops around. **SPRONG!**

I am green and brown, and as thin as a twig.

I have six long legs, and I hold my front legs close to me.

This makes it look like I'm praying.

Do you see me hidden?
Who am I?

I'M A
PRAYING MANTIS!

The praying mantis is a long and thin insect. It hunts without moving! It sits on a twig or a branch and blends in. When an insect passes by, the mantis quickly grabs it with its powerful front legs. **ZOWIE!** With its long, slender wings, it flies from one tree to another.

I might have big antlers, but I hide by standing still.

I am mostly brown, and the underside of my tail is white.

Running very fast and jumping high are what I do best!

Do you see me hidden?
Who am I?

I'M A DEER!

The white-tailed deer stays perfectly still when it senses trouble. It's much harder to spot this way. If danger comes near, it runs and holds up its tail, showing the bright white underside like a white flag. The deer is fast, like a car. It jumps over fallen trees and races away. **BOING!**

I'm big and burly, and my white fur matches the snow.

I live and hunt only where it's icy cold.

I have huge, sharp claws!
When I stand up, I'm very tall.

Do you see me hidden?
Who am I?

I'M A BEAR!

A **polar bear's** white fur helps it to blend into the snowy habitat. It doesn't need to hide because it's the largest hunter in the land. Other bears sleep all winter—but not the polar bear. It's most active during winter, when nights are long and dark. It doesn't eat much in summer while it awaits the return of wintry weather. **BRRR!**

CRITTER FACTS

Here's a great place to learn more extra-cool, fun facts about the critters featured in this book.

BURROWING OWL

The burrowing owl is the only type of owl that nests underground. It creates a burrow with a small room at the end. There, it lays its eggs right on the dirt. The young hatch in the dark den. The parents feed them large insects. Later in life, the young will also eat snakes, frogs, lizards and mice.

GRAY WOLF

The wolf is related to our pet dogs. Most gray wolves are gray in color, but many are black or white. Wolves hunt in packs for much larger animals, such as deer and moose. Pack members work with each other to provide enough food for their families.

SOUTHERN FLYING SQUIRREL

The Southern Flying Squirrel and Northern Flying Squirrel are the only flying squirrels in North America. The southern is much more common and smaller than the northern. They use loose flaps of skin along their sides to glide. There are lots of flying squirrels. We don't notice them because they stay in trees after dark and rarely come down to the ground.

AMERICAN ALLIGATOR

The American alligator lives in ponds, lakes and rivers. It is the largest reptile in North America. It walks slowly on land, but it can move fast in water. The tail is long and powerful and helps alligators to swim. The largest alligators tend to live alone. The younger ones are often found in groups.

BROWN CREEPER

The brown creeper has spotted brown feathers that blend in with tree bark. When a creeper senses a threat, such as a hawk, it stops moving. This makes it hard to see. To hunt, the creeper lands at the base of a large tree and climbs up the trunk. Along the way, it looks for hidden insects and insect eggs. Once it gets to the top of the trunk, it flies to a nearby tree and starts at the bottom again.

SHORT-TAILED WEASEL

Short-tailed weasels are sometimes called ermine or stoats. They change color from brown in summer to white in winter. Either way, they always have a black tip on their tails. Found nearly all over the world, they are among the smallest land predators on the planet. Males are larger than the females, though. They weigh about half a pound and are just six to twelve inches long!

BULLFROG

The bullfrog is our largest frog and lives in ponds, lakes and rivers. It eats everything from crayfish to dragonflies. It also has been known to eat small birds! With its large hind legs, it jumps great distances and swims through water very fast. Usually it lives alone, but in spring the males gather and call from shallow ponds. Most are green. Others are dark green to brown.

PRAYING MANTIS

The praying mantis is a common insect in some parts of North America. It has a funny name because it holds its legs as if in prayer when it hunts for food. The mantis has a large head that has the shape of a triangle. It can turn its head halfway around to see things all around. It has huge eyes and can see more colors than people can.

WHITE-TAILED DEER

White-tailed deer are the most common large mammals in North America. They can be found in a wide variety of habitats. Only the males have antlers. The antlers drop off each year, and then new ones grow. White-tailed deer are reddish brown in summer and light brown to gray in winter. Their name refers to the white fur under their tails.

POLAR BEAR

Polar bears are the largest land predators in the world. They eat mostly seals, which they catch on the ice in the far north. They live in Alaska, Canada, Greenland, Russia and Norway. Polar bears spend a lot of time swimming in the ocean. Their fur is actually clear, not white. A hollow core in the hairs makes the fur appear white.

Hiding Spots

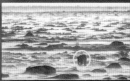

ABOUT THE AUTHOR

Stan Tekiela

Naturalist, wildlife photographer and writer Stan Tekiela is the author of more than 175 field guides, nature books, children's books, wildlife audio CDs, puzzles and playing cards, presenting many species of birds, mammals, reptiles, amphibians, trees, wildflowers and cacti in the United States. Stan has a Bachelor of Science degree in Natural History from the University of Minnesota, and he has received national and regional awards for his books and photography. You can follow Stan on Facebook and Twitter, and contact him at www.naturesmart.com.

More Children's Books from Stan

Stan Tekiela's books for children feature gorgeous photographs of real animals paired with captivating text. They introduce children to common, interesting and important types of North American animals.